In Celebration of

_____

_____

_____

_____

Date

Today is a very Special Day

Guests

Messages & Wishes

_____

_____

_____

_____

_____

_____

_____

_____

_____

_____

_____

Guests

Messages & Wishes

_____

_____

_____

Guests

Messages & Wishes

_____

_____

_____

_____

_____

_____

_____

_____

_____

_____

_____

_____

_____

_____

Guests

Messages & Wishes

_____

_____

_____

_____

_____

_____

_____

_____

_____

_____

_____

Guests

Messages & Wishes

Guests

Messages & Wishes

Guests

Messages & Wishes

_____

_____

_____

_____

_____

_____

_____

_____

_____

_____

_____

Guests

Messages & Wishes

_____

_____

_____

Guests

Messages & Wishes

_____

_____

_____

_____

_____

_____

_____

_____

_____

_____

_____

_____

Guests

Messages & Wishes

_____

_____

_____

_____

_____

_____

_____

_____

_____

_____

_____

_____

Guests

Messages & Wishes

_____

_____

_____

_____

_____

_____

_____

_____

_____

_____

_____

Guests

Messages & Wishes

Guests

Messages & Wishes

_____

_____

_____

_____

_____

_____

_____

_____

_____

_____

_____

_____

Guests

Messages & Wishes

Guests

_____

_____

_____

Messages & Wishes

_____

_____

_____

_____

_____

_____

_____

_____

_____

Guests

Messages & Wishes

Guests

Messages & Wishes

_____

_____

_____

_____

_____

_____

_____

_____

_____

Guests

Messages & Wishes

Guests

Messages & Wishes

_____

_____

_____

_____

_____

_____

_____

_____

_____

_____

_____

_____

Guests

Messages & Wishes

Guests

_____

_____

_____

Messages & Wishes

_____

_____

_____

_____

_____

_____

_____

_____

_____

Guests

Messages & Wishes

_____

_____

_____

_____

_____

_____

_____

_____

_____

_____

_____

_____

_____

Guests

Messages & Wishes

_____

_____

_____

_____

_____

_____

_____

_____

_____

_____

_____

_____

Guests

Messages & Wishes

Guests

_____

_____

_____

Messages & Wishes

_____

_____

_____

_____

_____

_____

_____

_____

Guests

Messages & Wishes

Guests

Messages & Wishes

Guests

Messages & Wishes

_____

_____

_____

_____

_____

_____

_____

_____

_____

_____

_____

Guests

Messages & Wishes

_____

_____
_____
_____
_____
_____
_____
_____
_____
_____

Guests

Messages & Wishes

Guests

Messages & Wishes

_____

_____

_____

_____

_____

_____

_____

_____

_____

_____

_____

_____

Guests

_____

_____

_____

Messages & Wishes

_____

_____

_____

_____

_____

_____

_____

_____

_____

Guests

Messages & Wishes

_____

_____

_____

_____

_____

_____

_____

_____

_____

_____

Guests

Messages & Wishes

_____

_____

_____

_____

_____

_____

_____

_____

_____

_____

_____

_____

Guests

Messages & Wishes

_____

_____

_____

_____

_____

_____

_____

_____

_____

_____

_____

Guests

Messages & Wishes

_____

_____

_____

_____

_____

_____

_____

_____

_____

_____

_____

_____

_____

Guests

_____

_____

_____

Messages & Wishes

_____

_____

_____

_____

_____

_____

_____

_____

_____

Guests

Messages & Wishes

Guests

Messages & Wishes

_____

_____

_____

_____

_____

_____

_____

_____

_____

_____

_____

Guests

Messages & Wishes

Guests

Messages & Wishes

_____

_____
_____
_____
_____

_____
_____
_____
_____

_____
_____
_____

Guests

Messages & Wishes

Guests

Messages & Wishes

_____

_____

_____

_____

_____

_____

_____

_____

_____

_____

_____

_____

Guests

Messages & Wishes

Guests

Messages & Wishes

_____

_____

_____

_____

_____

_____

_____

_____

_____

_____

_____

_____

Guests

_____

_____

_____

Messages & Wishes

_____

_____

_____

_____

_____

_____

_____

_____

_____

Guests

Messages & Wishes

_____

_____

_____

_____

_____

_____

_____

_____

_____

_____

Guests

Messages & Wishes

Guests

Messages & Wishes

_____

_____

_____

_____

_____

_____

_____

_____

_____

_____

_____

Guests

Messages & Wishes

_____

_____

_____

_____

_____

_____

_____

_____

_____

_____

Guests

Messages & Wishes

Guests

Messages & Wishes

Guests

Messages & Wishes

_____

_____

_____

_____

_____

_____

_____

_____

_____

_____

_____

Guests

Messages & Wishes

Guests

Messages & Wishes

_____

_____

_____

_____

_____

_____

_____

_____

_____

_____

_____

Guests

Messages & Wishes

Guests

Messages & Wishes

_____

_____

_____

_____

_____

_____

_____

_____

_____

_____

_____

_____

Guests

Messages & Wishes

Guests

Messages & Wishes

_____

_____

_____

_____

_____

_____

_____

_____

_____

_____

Guests

Messages & Wishes

Guests

Messages & Wishes

_____

_____

_____

_____

_____

_____

_____

_____

_____

_____

_____

Guests

Messages & Wishes

_____

_____

_____

_____

_____

_____

_____

_____

_____

_____

_____

Guests

Messages & Wishes

_____

_____

_____

_____

_____

_____

_____

_____

_____

_____

_____

Guests

Messages & Wishes

_____

_____

_____

_____

_____

_____

_____

_____

_____

_____

_____

_____

Guests

Messages & Wishes

_____

_____

_____

_____

_____

_____

_____

_____

_____

_____

_____

Guests

Messages & Wishes

_____

_____

_____

_____

_____

_____

_____

_____

_____

_____

_____

_____

_____

Guests

_____

_____

_____

Messages & Wishes

_____

_____

_____

_____

_____

_____

_____

_____

Guests

Messages & Wishes

_____

_____

_____

_____

_____

_____

_____

_____

_____

_____

_____

_____

Guests

Messages & Wishes

Guests

Messages & Wishes

Guests

Messages & Wishes

_____

_____

_____

_____

_____

_____

_____

_____

_____

_____

_____

Guests

Messages & Wishes

_____

_____

_____

_____

_____

_____

_____

_____

_____

_____

_____

_____

_____

Guests

Messages & Wishes

_____

_____

_____

_____

_____

_____

_____

_____

_____

_____

_____

_____

Guests

Messages & Wishes

_____

_____

_____

_____

_____

_____

_____

_____

_____

_____

_____

_____

Guests

Messages & Wishes

_____

_____

Guests

_____

_____

_____

Messages & Wishes

_____

_____

_____

_____

_____

_____

_____

_____

Guests

Messages & Wishes

_____

_____

_____

_____

_____

_____

_____

_____

_____

_____

_____

Guests

_____

_____

_____

Messages & Wishes

_____

_____

_____

_____

_____

_____

_____

_____

Guests

Messages & Wishes

_____

_____

_____

Guests

Messages & Wishes

Guests

Messages & Wishes

Guests

Messages & Wishes

_____

_____

_____

_____

_____

_____

_____

_____

_____

_____

_____

Guests

Messages & Wishes

_____

_____

_____

_____

_____

_____

_____

_____

_____

_____

_____

_____

Guests

Messages & Wishes

_____

_____

_____

_____

_____

_____

_____

_____

_____

_____

_____

_____

Guests

Messages & Wishes

_____

_____

_____

_____

_____

_____

_____

_____

_____

_____

_____

_____

Guests

Messages & Wishes

_____

_____

_____

_____

_____

_____

_____

_____

_____

_____

_____

Guests

_____

_____

_____

Messages & Wishes

_____

_____

_____

_____

_____

_____

_____

_____

_____

Guests

Messages & Wishes

_____

_____

_____

_____

_____

_____

_____

_____

_____

_____

_____

_____

Guests

Messages & Wishes

_____

_____

_____

_____

_____

_____

_____

_____

_____

_____

_____

Guests

Messages & Wishes

Guests

Messages & Wishes

_____

_____

_____

_____

_____

_____

_____

_____

_____

_____

_____

_____

Guests

Messages & Wishes

_____

_____

_____

_____

_____

_____

_____

_____

_____

_____

_____

Guests

Messages & Wishes

Guests

Messages & Wishes

_____

_____

_____

_____

_____

_____

_____

_____

_____

_____

Guests

Messages & Wishes

_____

_____

_____

_____

_____

_____

_____

_____

_____

_____

_____

Guests

Messages & Wishes

Guests

Messages & Wishes

_____

_____

_____

_____

_____

_____

_____

_____

_____

_____

_____

Guests

_____

_____

_____

Messages & Wishes

_____

_____

_____

_____

_____

_____

_____

_____

_____

Guests

_____

_____

_____

Messages & Wishes

_____

_____

_____

_____

_____

_____

_____

_____

Guests

Messages & Wishes

_____

_____

_____

_____

_____

_____

_____

_____

_____

_____

_____

_____

Guests

Messages & Wishes

_____

_____
_____
_____
_____
_____
_____
_____
_____

Guests

Messages & Wishes

_____

_____

_____

_____

_____

_____

_____

_____

_____

_____

_____

Guests

Messages & Wishes

_____

_____

_____

_____

_____

_____

_____

_____

_____

_____

_____

Guests

Messages & Wishes

Guests

_____

_____

_____

Messages & Wishes

_____

_____

_____

_____

_____

_____

_____

_____

Guests

Messages & Wishes

_____

_____

_____

_____

_____

_____

_____

_____

_____

_____

_____

Guests

Messages & Wishes

_____

_____

_____

_____

_____

_____

_____

_____

_____

_____

_____

Guests

Messages & Wishes

_____

_____

_____

Guests

Messages & Wishes

_____

_____

_____

_____

_____

_____

_____

_____

_____

_____

_____

Guests

Messages & Wishes

_____

_____

_____

_____

_____

_____

_____

_____

_____

_____

_____

Guests

Messages & Wishes

Guests

Messages & Wishes

Guests

_____

_____

_____

Messages & Wishes

_____

_____

_____

_____

_____

_____

_____

_____

_____

Guests

Messages & Wishes

Guests

Messages & Wishes

Guests

Messages & Wishes

Guests

Messages & Wishes

Guests

Messages & Wishes

Guests

Messages & Wishes

_____

_____

_____

_____

_____

_____

_____

_____

_____

_____

_____

_____

Guests

_____

_____

_____

Messages & Wishes

_____

_____

_____

_____

_____

_____

_____

_____

_____

Guests

Messages & Wishes

Made in the USA
Middletown, DE
13 June 2019